THE

JOURNEY

CONTINUES

ISBN-13: 978-1495399077

ISBN-10: 1495399079

We are all on a journey. A journey of discovery, whether it is a physical journey that takes us to the next street to see what is there or it takes us around the world. Then there is the inward journey of discovery. What do we find there?

In this the second book the journey continues. What we find here inside these pages may not be reality, but then again there some that are based on actual happenings. With others there may be some elements of the real world intruding. After all, all fantasy has a beginning in this world and it is how we see that reality that makes us shape the fantasy.

Once again come on this journey through a poets mind.

Here I would like to take the opportunity to thank Mariette van Galen once again for her unwavering help and encouragement she gave me during the writing of this book. Without her invaluable help this book would not have been possible.

The Journey Continues

Once again this quest I'm on
This journey ever onwards
The spirit calls to journey on
I'll follow where it leads me

Through twist and turns of mind and thought
And things that surround me
Whispered words of what to write
And their interpretation

You may see the same I see
And yet you see it different
I'm not right and you're not wrong
We all just differ

So on I'll plough to write my words
To see the world bit different
Maybe in my shoes you'll stand
My visions to be sharing

So journey on with me my friend
Across this minefield laid
Never knowing next step we'll take
Or what we find there

How The World Was Created
(or Gundahwandi)

Come with me to days gone past
Before the world was formed
I will tell you how it came about
The land and all the creatures

The sky was dark, no sun or stars
And nothing there below it
From out of nowhere came the snake
Twas Gundahwandi, Life Giver

From her mouth the stars spewed forth
Lighting up the heavens
From her belly she laid the eggs
It was the sun and the planets

Back and forth, round she slithered
All around she wove her magic
Plants and animals all came into being
And man her greatest creation

The deed was done, round she looked
All she saw pleased her
Was time for rest, her job was done
The rest was left for mankind

Secrets? What secrets?

What is this pain that wakes you
Why does this nightmare shake you
These demons coming to break you
And yet in silence suffering

Counting days slowly passing
Hiding screams that no one knows
Who is there to blame
For the pressure and pain

To look within for blame or fault
For their faces tell the story
They seek for truths that lay hidden
And truths they never find

Deadly Despair

This room so dark and dreary
Alone I sit in here
Anger, pain, despair and lies
This mantle around me sits

Where is this love you promised
The joy of life you said
Always here, never to leave
To be my one and only

To laugh at death while holding hands
A love so sweet and true
This room so dark and dreary
Alone I sit in here

My only friend a Forty five
Whispers quietly in my ear
Peace and calm and serenity
I will give to you

Kiss me now and say goodbye
And leave this world behind
A finger twitch, a shot rings out
And silence left behind

Come To Me

Come look at me, I hear you scream
Look deep into my eyes
What do you see lurking there?
Waiting to be found

Come listen to me, I hear you shout
Come listen to my words
What do they say? What do they tell?
What do you hear from me?

Come feel this heart, I hear you yell
This beating heart within
What does this rapid rhythm spell?
What meaning lays in this?

Come taste my love, I hear you whisper
Come closer near to me
And all I am and all I'll be
My love for you, my love

Quite Comfortably Numb

Ah you beautiful amber liquid
You're a pal to my soul
You take away, what can I say
This memory of pain

My head it spins, quite numb I think
I believe this feeling's bliss
What was this pain I'm thinking of
My mind is not quite clear

You're a drunk they say
Haaa! haaa! I laugh at them,
I'll drink to that, another one
Keep filling up my glass

And soon, I know, all pain will pass
And dreams will fade away
There I'll be, where I want to be
Quite comfortably numb

Don't We Learn

I hear the cry of the dead and wounded
Calling me cross time and space
The shadows littered with their bodies broken
And streets running red hot with blood

Killing all who dare speak against us
Those that share not our visions bright
The children young and oh so innocent
Their lives cut so very short

Those killing fields around the world
Bounded not by race or creed
Swords giving way to guns and cannons
Now the threat of germ warfare

Don't we learn from past mistakes
These spirits of the dead they cry
Listen now the time is coming
End of days is nigh upon us

My Version of Truth

My day is in such a daze
I know not what to do
All this beer and wine I drink
I just don't want to stop

You don't know the life I've had
It's this that makes me drink
I need to blur reality
To take away the pain

Two marriages I've had fail
My kids don't want to know me
They say their old man's a drunk
Ranting, raving and cussin'

A job it seems I cannot get
They just don't understand me
I need a drink to soothe my nerves
And get me through the day

I don't believe when people say
That I'm an alcoholic
I can stop, if I really want
But I enjoy my drinking

If sometimes truth is too blurred
And I can't tell the difference
So what, I don't really care
It's my version that matters

So I don't care, I'll carry on
And drink into oblivion
It's what I want that really counts
Anyway, I'm a heck of a nice fella

Words

Twisting, turning, squirming, yearning
Why can't they let me be
Cluttering, muttering, clanging and banging
What have they done to me

Over and over they run around
Dancing their little twirl
Put me this way, no, no, that way
Their song goes on and on

They jump around to tantalise
Here I look much better
Turn me round, now add this one
Is this the way you want us

So when they start to get too loud
I put my pen to paper
Write them down just like they sound
And get some peace till later

These Voices

I

Merciless these voices lash
Driving me insane
No hiding place is safe for me
They find me everywhere

I twist and turn down slippery paths
To hide within my mind
Yet still they follow on and on
No peace for me to find

They howl and scream
A banshees wail
Yet other times so gentle
Telling me what must be done
To satisfy the hunger

Blood more blood
The voices whisper
Blood more blood they scream
Merciless these voices lash
Driving me insane

II

Why, where, when, who, what
The voices assail me
From all sides
And I
Squirming 'neath their lashings
Know not what to say

These voices have
Not always been
They came from I know not where
Nor time, nor place
Constrains them
And compassion show they not

Life Worth Living

A leaf falls gently to kiss the ground
A newborn baby's wail

The dove of peace flies smoothly past
The smell of new mown grass

Damp earth with first rain drops
A lover's kiss with deep embrace

Rainbow arching across the sky
Setting of the Red sun

Ocean breeze, damp salt air
Flowers, colours all in bloom

Heavy fruit ripe on the trees
Children's laughter.....echoing

Joyous singing, rising high
This makes life worth living

A Moment In Time

Hanging by a moment in time
This moment stretched forever
Earth below me, sky above
Between them I am floating

Past my ears the wind is rushing
Setting up a fearful howl
Through the midst of clouds I travel
Journey's end seems closer now

Pulled the ripcord, nothing happened
Knew my time had finally come
Trees and houses so distinct now
See the house that I call home

Hanging by a moment in time
This moment stretched forever
I can hear the angels sing
Greeting me at heaven's gate

Forever Enigmatic

Silence reaching cross time and space

There to wait never knowing

Empty promises quickly made

Promises not meant for keeping

How and what, where and why

Answers not forthcoming

Never knowing, never seeing

Is this how it was meant to be

Eternity lasts forever

The Man Who Wouldn't Take No

Here he comes, it's time to hide
He'll nag me once again
"Have you talked to Jesus today?
It's time you got to know him"

"I really don't care," I'd answer him
"I'd appreciate if you quit it
This Jesus that you talk about
Doesn't mean a thing to me"

He'd only smile and start again
And tell me all these stories
Of miracles past and now
And how I need the healing

"Thank you now but I'm quite fine
And I don't need your Jesus
So go away and leave me alone
And find another sucker"

"A meeting we have this Sunday night
You really need to be there
This guest has come from overseas
He spreads the word of God now"

I'd had enough, I told him so
"I'll come this once, once only
And when I'm done you'll leave alone
And all this talk of Jesus"

Agreement made, I went along
The church was really packed inside
People singing, dancing and praising
Their worship appeared so joyful

The preacher man he came and spoke
About Jesus and salvation
Of how he died to give us life
And entrance into Heaven

Let all who need Jesus now
Come down for a blessing
Jesus wants to share His love
And assure your place in Heaven

My body rose by spirit hands
And guided down my footsteps
Peace and calm and lovingness
Followed the preacher's prayer

Jesus came into my heart
And changed my life forever
Blessed be my friend called Ron
Who wouldn't take no for an answer

In memory of Ron Hadcroft, a great man that I was honoured
to call friend.

Is This The Day

Her eyes bored into mine
And hot breath on my cheek
I could feel the heat of her body
Through the thin cotton blouse

Her breath came rapid
As her arms encircled me
Her body against me tightly pressed
Raising my expectations

I could hear my blood
Pounding in my ears
Driving me to distraction

Was this the day
My life would change
Or was I merely dreaming

X – Y x Z + T = M

Time sits heavily on my mind

Reverberating across time and space

Allowing echoes to cross the void

Visions flashing across the sky

Iridescent lights floating and dipping

Slowly my mind becoming numb

Allowing strange thoughts to creep in

Loosening my hold on reality

Before too long I am gone

Exploring all this madness

Return I cannot, I've lost my way

Today will last forever

All Tis Well This Morning

Sun dappled shadows dancing across the ground
While leaves rustling to the gentle breeze
Whispering their secrets to the trees
And the trees swaying ever so slowly
Nodding their branches in agreement

Flowers their faces turned to the sun
Their happy wide open smiles
Drinking in the joy that surrounds them
And multi coloured birds swooping between the trees
Performing their dance on currents of air

Nearby the brook merrily gurgles
As it passes through the glen
And all around nature's song
All tis well this morning

Last Dying Breath

When you walked out you took the sun
The moon and the stars with you
You left an empty void where the screams
Of my despair disappear into nothingness

Again and again and again I call but
There is no answer, for you are gone
I am only met with the utter silence
Of my lack of understanding

What have I done to bring about this
This desolation within my heart
This knife that pierces my breast
And draws forth my life blood

And even with my dying breath
I still cling to the last memory of you

Inside Me

You look at me what do you see
A body bent, misshapen
Features slack with drooling mouth
And fingers constant twitching

The only sounds my mouth escapes
Are grunts that sound so pig like
Body trapped in chair on wheels
No way for me to move it

But spare a thought for me inside
This body that I'm trapped in
My mind is clear, yes I can think
Inside of me I'm normal

I too have hopes, dreams and wishes
Yet no-one I can tell
A prisoner I am of my appearance
Stuck inside this shell of living hell

Quietly, Softly, Gently

Quietly, softly, gently, a heart beats at night
A lonely heart, an aching heart
One filled with pain and fears

Quietly, softly, gently, I weep in the night
Aching, breaking, my pillow soaked with tears

Quietly, softly, gently, You tiptoe in my room
You hold my hand, stroke my brow, whisper 'I love you'

Quietly, softly, gently, you wipe away my tears
Blessed grace, saving grace, flowing through and through

Quietly, softly, gently, I drift off to sleep
Saving love, covering love, my Jesus watches me

I Hear

I hear the song of morning birds
And wings I wish to spread
To fly up high where troubles naught
Are apt to pass you by

I hear the song of a church choir
Singing praises to the Lord
My soul it lifts and soars aloft
Like an eagle on the wing

I hear the wind through trees it rush
To places far away
My memories lift and swirl about
The lifetime of my past

I hear a heavy laboured breath
And heart that beats so slow
My time is here, I go with joy
And Heaven waits for me

For to Give Me Life

You have plucked the sun from the sky
And lit up my life

The stars from the heavens
For to make me a crown

The warm trade winds as a mantle
To keep me warm all day

Waters from the clear mountain stream
For to quench my thirst

The moon from its path at night
So that I might find my way to you

My heart back from the darkness
For to give me life

The Hermit

Alone he lives with no friend or foe
Far from civilisation
Animals come and eat from his hand
Know the gentle soul within him

A rough bark hut for shelter he has
And leaves to make his bedding
Roots and berries for food he'll take
For meat's not part of his diet

His clothes are tattered, torn to shreds
And reeking of stale urine
A heavy coat his pride and joy
To keep at bay cold winter

This gentle soul would do no harm
To neither man nor beast
All he asks from anyone
To be left in isolation

Depths of Despair

A cave so deep and dark and dank
Is where I want to be
No light to shine, no breath to stir
To hide myself from thee

My sins upon my neck I wear
A chain that weighs me down
Grief, anger, pity, hate
My bedding they do make

A voice it whispers in my head
Love, forgiveness, it does speak
Open your heart and open your eyes
Let the light shine in

Dare I hope, Dare I believe
After all I've done, all I have been
Words spoken, acts committed
That someone cares for me

Thou Art Like

(by Willie Shake the Spear)

Thou art like the winter's night
Cold and frosty and full of fight

Thou art like the spring's rain
Wet, bothersome and a real pain

Thou art like the summer's sun
Too hot but never ready for fun

Thou art like the meadow's brook
I want loving, you're always crook

Thou art like the snow on mountain high
I hold you, gone in the blink of an eye

Thou art like the Devil's spawn
So goodbye to you Evonne

What is Love

What is love I shout out loud?
But no-one here will answer

What is love I ask the clouds?
But they just keep on drifting

What is love I ask the sun?
But it's rays just keep on warming

What is love I ask the moon?
But it looks down uncaring

What is love I ask myself?
And so many answers I'm getting

Death In The Fast Lane

I try to move but find I can't
There is blackness all around me
Sound I hear but not quite clear
Can't make out what they're saying

Where am I? how did I get here?
I cannot think of an answer
All I know is I can't see a thing
I can't even feel my body

Words I hear but sound so muffled
Sounds keep drifting in and out
If only I could remember
But only blackness stares back at me

Seems there's something at edge of memory
Remember party wild and free
Too much booze and too much smoking
I was smashed beyond belief

Oh my God! now I remember
Driving home was drunk too much
Coming round that blasted corner
Lost control and drifted off

Round and round, seemed forever
Over and over rolled the car
Tracey screaming in pain and terror
Smelling petrol, fire crackling

Feel the heat and panic rising
Desperate to get out of there
Smell of human flesh burning
Blackness claimed the rest of night

Here it is four years later
Blindness is for rest of life
My body burned so badly
Lucky to be even alive

Many days I sit at graveside
Talk to Tracey all day long
Lost my Love, my life companion
Burdened with guilt I carry on

King Of The Hill

I have reached the pinnacle
I'm the King of the hill
All pleasures at my command
Not a thing money can't buy

Mansion built atop the hill
And fast cars in the stable
Choice of women every night
And servants all around me

And yet there's something wrong with life
I fear there's something missing
Inside of me a hunger burns
And I don't know how to quench it

Loneliness it creeps in on me
While surrounded by all this splendour
I look for friends yet friends are none
Only people who fear my power

And what if time for death is near
How will I fare then
There's something all my money can't buy
Will somebody tell me please

Black Dog

Still days there are
When the Black Dog visits
On days that I'm alone
Those days I question myself
What have I done wrong

It's then I feel so useless
Though right I've tried to do
Yet still this feeling hits me
And Black Dog comes around
He shows no peace or compassion
I keep fighting this fight alone

Round and round my thoughts go
Down a spiral staircase
Ever deeper I am sinking
In the mire of my delusions
My nerve ends screaming
'Stop! No more! Enough.'
But I'm not listening
The black dog has a hold on me

The What's His Name Show

Oh dear, my mistake
The TV I turned on
Just my luck to get that show
Called the 'What's His Name Show'

You know the one I'm talking about
Where guests their dirty linen air
Wives confront their cheating men
And men their sluttish wives

I've come to tell you I'm a man
The trannie conceited struts
While devastated the boyfriend sits
His world just fell apart

Fat whore likes to show her body
Takes clothes off to show her rolls
All the audience laughing at her
She can't see she's just a joke

Boyfriend dances onto stage
Looks so cute with bra and panties
Girl thinks what the hell has happened
How can I face my family at home

Ring the bell and come out fighting
Rip the clothes off, show them boobs
Audience chants, all excited
Egg them on to do even more

Strippers seductively gyrate
While pimps sit gloating by
And mothers weep to see their kids
Debase themselves this way

No depravity is too vile
To showcase on this show
Incest and things taboo
Presented as the norm

Oh Sodom and Gomorrah
Though once you were destroyed
It seems you've been resurrected
On the 'What's His Name Show'

Abuse

Part I
(One Time Too Many)

Who is this stranger staring back at me
Black eyes, bruised face, I do not know her
This could not be me, surely not again
He promised me so faithfully, never again

Yet here I was, the pain all too real
All over my body aching, breasts so tender
From violent punching, although I tried in vain
Even on the floor his boots did damage

All the while from his mouth spewed hatred
All my fault, drove him to it, or so he claims
Not content with just this bloody violence
Threw me down across a chair, raped me there

Took me harshly, brutally, with not a care
Can still feel the agony, many hours later
Try to rid myself of this clinging dirt feeling
But it feels like it is part of me

Begged for forgiveness, like he always does
He promised me so faithfully, never again
This is one time, one time too many
Picked up the phone, dialled the police

Part II
(The Continuation)

I imagine him grovelling at my feet
Begging me not to have him jailed
For once in his life he is scared
Gone is his cockiness
His domineering manner

All the times he beat and raped me
Said it was his due as my husband
I had to submit to his whim
All my tears and pleas
They just spurred him on

Now he is the one frightened
What will they do to him in jail
He is what they call a 'pretty boy'
Smouldering eyes, handsome
His soul does not match the outer

Mercy? I begged for mercy
I received none from him
Why should I show him some
He will only revert to his old self
I know I would be a victim again

NO! Not this time, not again
I smile as I watch him
Tears covering his face
Terror reflecting from his eyes
Utter hopelessness as I slam the door

I have cut off his last lifeline
Cast him adrift, rejected him
No longer someone to be controlled
Stood up to him and faced him down
Found my inner strength

As I lay in my bed tonight
I wrap my arms around me
Cocooning myself in warmth, security
Knowing that I am finally safe
Secure, unable to be hurt

A smile plays around the corners of my mouth
Now he is going to find out what it is like
What it is like to be beaten and raped
To be treated like something less than human
To be treated like someone's bitch

Part III
(Horses Ass)

I can't believe what happened, happened
The judge so stern and sober sitting there
Wagged his finger through the air

"This is unacceptable," with voice deep and sombre
"women are not there for hitting
There is no excuse I must say."

With these words spoken clearly
Pondering verdict with chin on hand
Here I thought justice was coming
For all the abuse I've endured

How many years will the judge give him
For all the broken bones I've had
To right the wrongs that he has done
The judge coughed and looked around
To let all see that he was ready

"I have given clear consideration
Of the remorse that you have shown
This time I will give you warning
Should I see you here again
I will have no hesitation
Inside of jail you then will see."

As he walked free from the Courtroom
Blew a kiss across the aisle
Is this what you call justice?
The law is nothing but a horses ass

Part IV
(No More)

I look in the mirror and what do I see
Who is this demon staring back at me
What happened to the nice girl I used to be

You opened my chest, ripped it apart
From within you tore out my heart
You laughed, you thought you were so smart

The knife I slipped into your chest
Deeper and deeper in I pressed
I sent you on to your eternal rest

Blood is splattered up the wall
And along the floor out to the hall
That's as far as you managed to crawl

So here I wait I'm sure they'll come
I've stopped thinking, my mind is numb
It was the demon that made me succumb

The Three Little Pigs – A New Story

Now here's a tale that needs to be told
Of three little pigs so very different
Their names were Ernest, Roger and Winky
These names by their parents were given

Now I could say these pigs were not so nice
At times they were rightly a pain in the ass
Their parents had given up all hope
Of taming those three terrible pigs

All Ernest wanted was to watch TV
All day and night cartoons he'd see
Should anything happen he'd scream and cry
And run berserk throughout the house

Now Roger was different from other two
He was dirty and messy and stank a treat
His nose was runny and boogers on clothes
And socks not parted from feet for years

Winky you'd think sounds rather nice
But of all of them he was the worst
His toys he'd throw all over the house
And toilet seat he'd firmly leave down

Now mother pig when nature called
Her bottom she did plant
A mighty scream, a yell so loud
'Yuck!! my bottom is now all sticky

Those dirty little pigs,' she yelled
'They piddled all over the seat again
This is so bad, I'm sick of it
Please we need to find an answer'

They pondered to, they pondered fro
You could almost hear them thinking
Hope was almost given up
When the answer suddenly struck them

Away from home they would move
Across the road to his mother
There the pigs would not find them
To cross the street was not allowed them

On his way coming home
A trailer papa pig rented
To load all things from in house
Across the street to be moving

The beds, the lounge, all dining room
And even the TV was loaded
Not a thing was left behind
Except three cups, plates and spoons

Off they set across the road
A new life for them awaited
Left behind all sorrows and woes
Three little pigs now on their own

Home they came from school all bright
Ready for some mischief
When shock, horror, oh my gosh
They found the house quite empty

Ernest went to sit down
No lounge to rest his body
Worse things were yet to come
No cartoons and no TV to watch them

Winky walked round and round
No toys to be found here
How could he throw them round the house
If there were no toys to be found there

Roger didn't really care
His stink was always with him
The only thing that upset him
No toilet seat to pee on

Just then a mighty bang on the door
The pigs jumped and squealed with fright
'Who's there?' they cried so timidly
'Tis Wolfred your friendly salesman'

'Open the door and let me in
I'll show you wonders and excitement'
'Do you have a TV with cartoons on it?'
Yelled the pig called Ernest

'The things I have you'll surely like
So let me in you pigs so tasty'
'No! no,' they cried in unison
'Not by the hair on our chinny, chin, chin'

This made the saleswolf mighty mad
He raved, ranted and shouted
'You wait pigs till I get in
A fine dinner you'll be making'

He pounded and pounded on the door
So hard they could hear it cracking
Suddenly it broke right in
There was a wolf of immense proportions

Now Ernest being ever so dumb
Asked 'have you got a TV?'
Wolf picked him up, one mighty gulp
And Ernest was gone forever

Now Winky knew trouble was here
Was looking for some place for hiding
The wolf just laughed as he picked him up
And ate this tasty morsel

Roger was thinking mighty quick
He was too young to be dinner
A sock parted from his foot
One deft move, in wolf's mouth shoved it

The wolf coughed, chocked and spluttered
Both little pigs were spat out
One last gasp and twitch of limbs
The wolf had met his maker

There is a moral to this tale
Or so I've been told
To softly always walk in life
And a BIG stink to be carrying

Putting Pen To Paper

Here I sit with pages blank
Of what to write I wonder
Should it be of lovers lost
Or ones that found each other

Possibly into outer space
And different worlds found there
Blaze across the evening sky
My retro rockets firing

Or deep beneath this earth's crust
Descending deeper ever deeper
So far down where light don't shine
Down where Morlocks are living

How about beneath ocean waves
Far down to Atlantis City
Civilisation that once was lost
Now newly rediscovered

So many choices, I just don't know
This blank sheet still stares at me
What to write I wish I knew
Putting pen to paper

Tomorrow The Sun Might Return

Yesterday I felt I was on top of the world
It would seem that nothing could go wrong
Or so I thought, you know famous last words
The sun so bright, a gentle cooling breeze
Enough to dry the sweat upon my brow
There I sat and watched the sea roll in
The white caps merrily chasing one another
Like colts chasing each other cross the meadow
And then they would crash upon the shore
With each attempt getting closer to me
And there I sat, with beer in hand
It seemed the world my oyster

That was yesterday, before I went to bed
I woke up to a dull, grey, sunless day
No songs of birds that I could hear
Just a nerve wracking screeching of something
Some type of bird, I know not what
Nor do I really care, it's all the same
It seemed that while I slept despair rained down
It soaked me, covered me from head to toe
Despair oozed out of my every pore
My life had gone the way of the outhouse
Utter despair, like the very depths of hell

I wished my life, it was no life, would end
Every sound I heard was dull and lifeless
Food was dreary, lifeless and without taste
Why even the very air that I breathed
Tasted like it had passed through a crypt
With the rotten stench of death on it
You could almost taste the flesh eating maggots
The walls, the walls that I had come to love
Whispered to me, what good are you
No-one wants you, end it now, no-one cares
And yet, I still cling to life with finger tips
Not quite ready, not yet, still hanging on
For who knows, tomorrow the sun might return

Little Red Riding Hood

It was last night
In the dark of night
With candle glowing

I held her tight
Little Red Riding Hood
Savouring the moment

I licked my lips
I brought her close
Such a heady aroma

I could not wait
I made her mine
The taste so heavenly

One gulp, she was gone,
Gone was my Red Riding
Resistance was futile

So please kind Sir
I'll have another
Pour another Red Riding

1 oz gin
3/4 oz creme de mure
3/4 oz wild strawberry liqueur
1 1/2 oz orange juice

Shake and strain into a double-cocktail glass filled with
crushed ice. Garnish with berries, a short straw, and serve.

Distant Memory

Fire runs through my veins
And pain twists and turns
No matter where I run or hide
It always seems to find me

On my knees I pray to what?
Something must be out there
I know not is it god or what
Maybe some universal spirit

Seems that whatever is out there
Does not pay attention
For on and on goes this pain
Heartache and awful loneliness

Into the void I shout my agony
Silence is all that to me returns
Silence so loud it deafens me
Now I know I am alone

Tears that drip upon the ground
Are gone to show no passing
Will I be like my salty tears
Nothing, not even a memory

Mind's eye sees the tracks
And blood slowly welling
Has it come to this? no hope
No pain and no redemption

A sign I ask, just a sign
To set feet in different direction
I wait in vain for no-one cares
Not even the so called almighty

And as my life slowly drains
A mantle of peace surrounds me
Finally this awful pain
This pain becomes a distant memory

A Bit Of Australian Slang

Strewth mate, you sprung me fair
I was just having a sickie
The weather's nice to go for swim
So grabbed me cossies and spare daks

Behind I left the little Vegemites
The missus there to mind them
Jumped into me Kingswood and bugger me
The bloody thing was on the blink

Fair dinkum mate, I tell no lie
I'm not one who wants to skite
The trouble and strife came out to fix
With hammer banged under the bonnet

'Give it a burl' she soon yelled
And blow me the old girl started
Quick as a wink I'm off you see
The big drink is calling me

So here I am with the rank and file
Trying to have a bit of peace
Now with all the trouble that I've had
You give me my walking papers

Mate, I think you're off your trolley
So take your job and just quietly
You can shove it where the sun don't shine

Your Highness

"Your Highness," says he as he bows low to the ground,
So low that his forehead almost scrapes it.
"I am but your utter most humble servant
To do what benefits and pleases your gloryness."
These words he spoke so slippery and oily
That should you step on them you would surely slip.
"Yes, yes, I know that you're here to serve me.
To grant my wishes as I ask, nay my demands,
But what I ask is your reward for service such as this?"
"A trifling, a whimsy, mere bagatelle, not much at all,
This paper sign, it gives me right to something,
Something worth nothing at all, not even a cent.
It is merely your soul, it is of no use to you.
To be honest it's of no use to me, but you see
They look good on my mantle piece and there they sit.
So really you see, I give so much to you
And take but nothing of any worth in return
There is the deed, here is the pen, sign on the line."
The man pondered, eyes glinting with greed
To have the world at his feet, Emperor of all around
The pen he took, signed his name, done was the deed
"A wise choice, the world will know your name.
All will tremble and all will fear, yours is the world."
One last bow and one last scrape and gone in a puff
Left behind was a sulphur stench and smoke in the air.

The Prince And The Angels

It seems there was not long ago
A prince and all his angels
They sallied forth to ride around
To investigate earth's problems

They rode north to ice cold lands
Amongst the snow, sleet and hail
On they searched, even under rocks
But find something they did not

They turned around and south they rode
To climates so much warmer
To places where the sun shone bright
But answers none forthcoming

They rode towards the rising sun
Through streams and up the mountains
There they stood on top of the world
But not finding what they were seeking

Once again off they set
With view of sun slowly setting
This was last chance's hope
And yet their hope was forsaken

So much pain and so much grief
The prince stood there dejected
All around his angels wailed
To see this earth's suffering

What must he do to make us see
To stop what we are doing
Bring joy back to the prince
And have his angels rejoicing

Old Age

You look at me, your fingers point
Behind my back you laugh at me
And some of you are less than kind
To my face you call me names

I might be old and a bit infirm
My bones creak and I stagger a bit
The muscles weak, I'm not as strong
It happens as you get older

But you who laugh and point at me
I too once was young as you
I thought that youth was always mine
And never would age catch up with me

Seems to me that behind the door
And other dark hiding places
Old age was there hiding behind
Waiting to out come creeping

So laugh away and point at me
For old age is waiting for you
Then you might remember days of youth
When it's your turn for others to point at

Golden Spire

I see the spire golden bright
It points, this way home
My heart it beats faster now
Nine more K's to go
Waiting there my love, my life
The one I love the most

Travelling Through These Eerie Woods

Travelling through the eerie woods
Trees of bright red Granderwood
Beneath my feet the Grovel Grubs
Their marching sounds my ears do reach
Beware, beware, on them do not step
For their teeth gnaw through boots
And toes they find so very delicious

Above so high the treetops sway
Home to the green Karpunzels
So shrill their cry, a mating call
They are cannibalistic by nature
Should the time be wrong, no mating game
The battle is on, survival the game
The loser becomes this nights dinner

In the sky circling high above
The purple Diving Quarker Bird
Circles high and folds his wings
And dives to forest floor below
There he finds the tiny Lousacrats
Scurrying in panic to evade his dive
Those once caught, carried home for sharing

So I'm telling you, travel lightly my friend
Round every tree is lurking danger
Some are big and so easily seen
Yet some the danger's much smaller
So take care, my friend beware
You're travelling these woods so eerie
God be willing, these woods you'll be leaving

This Ghastly Depression

In the dark of night
When the moon is ripe
And loneliness my companion
Sad songs drifting sounding tripe
Fuelling my ghastly depression

There I sit watching misery
Spider walking up the wall
Whisky bottle brings memories
Memory takes me to a dance hall

There I met her tall and blonde
A vision so divine
Our eyes met was love's sight
I had to make her mine

Love blossomed, was like a dream
Was all that I'd prayed for
Together we would build our life
All that I wanted and more

Day came that we wed
Our vows we did speak
Man and wife we did become
And love grew from week to week

Word came I did not want
My heart ripped from my chest
A driver drunk, took her life
And I had to put her to rest

Darkness closed in all around
Was nothing left to live for
What I cherished, all was gone
And life is but a whore

In the dark of night
When the moon is ripe
And loneliness my companion
Sad songs drifting sounding tripe
Fuelling my ghastly depression

Death In A Coal Mine (Child Miners)

Into the bowels of the earth we descend
Down into the pit of hell
Crawling on hands and knees to mine
This precious fuel they call coal

Now Petey and I we are almost men
He is ten and I'm eleven
Been working here, down this mine
These last two years and month now

Mum is counting on us as men
Since Dad died from consumption
Coughed every night, spat out blood
Now gone to be with Jesus

The work is hard, it's hot down here
To work by flickering candlelight
The dust so thick, you always taste it
It makes you cough and splutter

We've almost reached the coal face
When I can hear some rumbling
I turned my head to speak to Petey
When the world collapsed around me

I don't know how long I lay there
When sense returned to me
By the flickering light I could see
The roof caved in behind me

Now I don't know if Petey was safe
Or if Petey was buried under
But what I knew and the news was bad
This was a miner's worst nightmare

Not a breeze came through, no fresh air
The tunnel tightly sealed
I think I knew deep in my heart
My bones would find rest here

Time passed, don't know how long
The candle burned away
The last light my eyes did see
Then blackness all around

I had seen night and I'd seen black
But never before black like this
The silence too was deafening
A tear squeezed from my eye

I cannot cry, I am a man
But the tears slid down my cheeks
I told myself for Mum I cried
What will become of her

The air so stale, tis hard to breathe
My eyelids heavy, drooping
Slowly I drift off to sleep
Tomorrow I'll awake in heaven

The Flying Dutchman

The wind through the rigging howled
As we were tossed about
Waves so high you could be buried at sea
To the bottom sunk in a trice

Fools we were to be out here
To think, outrun the weather
Caught we were in the storm of storms
These waves as high as mountains

But on we sailed, now too late
Our only hope was prayer
Myself I lashed to the wheel
To steer us out of trouble

My wife and child before my eyes
Gave reason for this battle
The crew they too had families
For them all I was trying

My eyes sore from all the spray
Was this some sort of imagination
What other ship would be fool enough
On a day like this to out venture

Yet there she was, all fully rigged
Sailing against the weather
It seemed there were no souls aboard
The ship ghostly in appearance

As she drew close to me
I could see the crew aboard her
Twas skeletons dressed in rags
With the Captain giving orders

On passing I could hear the wails
Begging and pleading for mercy
The stench that came from the passing ship
A smell so rotten and putrid

I prayed to all the gods I knew
That we would not be just like her
There are some things worse than death
And one had just passed me

How we managed to survive the night
I have no understanding
Came break of day the weather changed
The rest was fair weather sailing

We entered port and went our way
Not one word of this was spoken
Survived we had, our luck held
Would break if of this was spoken

And to this day I still recall
As I smoke my pipe by fire
Chills still run up and down my spine
The ghostly ship with the deathly crew

As The Bell Struck High Noon

Was so long ago, lost in the mists of time
Barely remember it, I must be getting old
WBut one thing I do know, should not have happened
Time heals all wounds, maybe even this one

She came from, no-one knew where
Settled down here, like a princess divine
Cast her eyes longing, over all the men
Married or not, mattered not to her

Conquests piled up, I could write a book
Left hearts shattered, families broken up
No-one could stop her, no-one immune
She lived life like a devil's spawn

To town came a preacher, young, tall, handsome
She wanted him, more than all the rest
Wile after wile, none seemed to work
Time after time he turned her down

The more he refused, the more she wanted
Her appearance slowly it changed
To be refused, never happened before
Desperation etched her face

To her be denied, then no-one have him
A plan was hatched, doom was sealed
To hell she'd take him, together they'd go
Then hers he'd be forevermore

In the midst of day, was almost high noon
In the street she met him with rifle in hand
A single shot, backward he flung
Was enough to send him heaven bound

A look around, more she saw
Five more quick shots, bridal party secured
A bullet for her, blew out her heart
As she lay there dying a smile lit her face

Seven dead as the bell struck high noon
A wedding day, the devil presides
What a sad day, is best forgotten
This day should be lost in the mists of time

Alzheimers

Inside of me, the place I live
This place so sad and lonely
No matter where I seek to find
There's nothing there for finding
I look in corners dark and dusty
And beneath the floors of wood
There is no furniture, all's bare
No curtains on my windows
From room to room down passageways
I drift, I aimlessly wander
There is nothing here to recognise
This place seems totally empty
Light that comes through window panes
Seems dull and unforgiving
And when I look out into the world
There is strangeness all around me
Not a face or word I recognise
Nothing there I remember
I wonder what do you see
When in my eyes you look
I hear the words, there's no-one home
But I don't know their meaning

The Poets Words

A poets words are powerful
They can gnaw on your insides
And set your heart ablaze
Or they can douse the flames
Of joy, peace and contentment
And bring pain, sorrow and suffering
These words can be truth
And set you free
Or they can be lies
To enslave you in their passions
Beware of the words of the poet
For they twist and they turn
And have the sting of an scorpion
Beware as to where they lead you
Maybe to a foreign country
Or one as strange as can be
Maybe even in another galaxy
But one thing is sure
Once these words have been read
You will never be the same
For the words of the poet
They will transform you

The Last Farewell

To thee I sing a song of farewell
Tis time for me to move on
These many nights together we spent
To me was the best of the best

So why? you ask, do I move on
Tis the bug called Wanderlust
And even though my heart breaks apart
It's onward I must go

Will I come back? your eyes ask me
Would love to say yes I will
But truth be known, as always will
This way I shan't pass again

So lift your glass for one more drink
And a last kiss for the road
Turn away, I'll hide my tears
As I leave this last time

Not one look, not a glance back
Just the blurry vision ahead
Even I don't know why I do what I do
And the lonely road stretches ahead

Death's Bell Chime

You think you can dream your dreams
While I labour at just living
You who plot all your schemes
And never think of giving

You walk past the beggar's hand
With not a second look
Poverty you believe should be banned
As you quote from a holy book

You ignore the pleas of sick and dying
A mantle of righteousness you wrap around
So holy are you, you hear no crying
So certain are you, you're heaven bound

But let me tell you loud and clear
That when you stand at Pearly gates
When you see Heaven so close, so near
That you will be in dire straits

I know thee not, be away with thee
For you have not loved me at all
No matter which way you might phrase your plea
It is down to Hell you will fall

So think while there is still time
To change the way that you act
Once you hear the death's bell chime
Then too late for deeds to retract

Merry Christmas

This sound I hear upon the roof
What could it possibly be
Could it be the reindeer hooves
Or Santa's gliding sleigh

This noise so strange drives me insane
With wonder and suspense
I need to look yet dare I not
What if my hopes are dashed

So quietly I sneak on roof
Up on this building so tall
What do I see, some one's up here
I jump and yell surprise

The look of shock upon his face
As slowly he tumbled backwards
And off the roof he fell so quick
To hit the ground with thud so sickening

What had I done? Down there he
Moaning, groaning, looking ever so sad
With left leg bent oh so queer
Oh my God, I've caused this trouble

Poor Santa's leg is broken
Tonight there'd be no presents
The ambulance took Santa away
To the hospital they whisked him

They'd fix him up, I'm sure they will
But I'm deep in this mess
If people find out what I had done
I think they might lynch me

So please forgive, I did not mean it
Have a Merry Christmas
And if no presents beneath the tree
Just think, it's the thought that counts

Damn It's Hot Down Here

Part I

Damn it's hot down here, much hotter than it should be
Flames licking up the walls and dancing round my toes
Sweat pouring down my back and soaking all my clothes
Everything that I touch is so damn hot adding to my woes

There he stood with horns on head and a sneer on his face
Furry legs stomping to unheard rhythm tapping cloven hooves
Sneer turns to amused grin, which turns to downright laughter
To see the shock that I was in, Hell is real, this it proves

He bowed quite low with demonic grin and in I was invited
He couldn't wait to show me round, Hell being his domain
He lead me here, and there, each place worse than the other
In everything was a design, a design for causing untold pain

He danced around with such delight, a demon's mad jig
Here I'll be for eternity, this place that God has forsaken
To suffer pain like none before and screams to last eternal
Oh how I wish that this was a dream and I would awaken

Damn It's Hot Down Here

Part II (On Probation)

It seemed to be an eternity that I've been down here
This pain I could not describe, it appears never ending
My body twisted this way and that, ever so contorted
I begged and pleaded to no avail for the devil was unbending

But then came the day, the day he came to see me
A chance for me to leave here, for me he'd make a deal
The only thing I'd have to do is bring more souls to him
This I thought that I could do and finally end my ordeal

Agree I did so quickly, lest he might change his mind
I would take the soul of anyone, for freedom I want to seek
Anything to get out of here, any soul I'd happily take
While I'm here no hope at all, my future looked real bleak

Came the day he let me free with harvest tools in bag
There was money, sex and more of these, all for temptation
The souls they came in multitudes, it was almost too easy
But I knew not to slacken off for I was still on probation

Damn It's Hot Down Here

Part III (Out of Hell)

I'm out this hell, I shall not fail, souls I'll be bringing
I don't care who or where, My own granny I'll be selling
Now you might think that this is bad and I should be stopping
But I'll tell you now, no way, no how, in hell will I be dwelling

So stand back, look out world, souls I'll be harvesting
If you get in my way, on the dotted line you'll sign
The more I get, the safer I'll feel, no more going back
I will laugh to see you suffer while I'm on cloud number nine

Hey you there, yes you, come see what I have for you
Do you want money or power, girls hanging all around
Whatever it is, your heart's desire, I will have for you
But beware my friend, there is a price, your soul hell bound

You'll cry and beg, plead all you will, I admit so did I
But nothing you do will matter at all, on the line you signed
The devil he will dance as he tortures your soul
For your greed you'll pay, as this world you leave behind

Damn It's Hot Down Here

Part IV (Freedom)

I think I'm close, my freedom won, so many sent to hell
I told you lies, you signed the deed, to hell you did descend
All the promises, all the lies, not one did come true
Too late you found the devil lies, too late to make amends

I've lost the count, the thousands sent on their way to doom
At night I hear in mind's ear the screams go round and round
I tell myself the fault is theirs, for sake of greed they signed
Once signed, no change of mind for now they were bound

So sing my friends and merry make, one more to the list
That's all I need for freedom's sake and free I will be
The devil's deed I have in hand, was hard to win from him
See him still a smirking look and quivering black goatee

So my friends below this poem I've left a line for you
Be so kind to sign on line and then to add your name
I promise I will think of you as I sip my cold white wine
And I will think that now you're gone, what a sad, sad shame

Where The Poets Reside

I heard the bell
Was loud and clear
A place where there is nothing to fear

On we went
Through dark of night
With joy towards dawn's first light

We wrote and wrote
Words that flowed
By any light that we found

And what we wrote
For all to read
Was words to amaze and astound

Lovers swooned
And lovers cried
For love completed and love denied

As sun arose
We dimmed our lights
Our separate paths we treaded

In The Cellar

The noise in the cellar becomes so loud
The snuffling and huffling, growling and all
Shut up, I yelled down this tiny opening
Tonight you'll be dining on white bread and water

The noises they turned from anger to sorrow
With pleading and begging and lots of I'm sorry
Now my heart was cold and turned to stone
Not once did I care for what was below

Not once, not twice but so many times gone past
I warned her over and over what her actions bring
She laughed, kept going, made life a misery
Now under my floor in the cellar she is

Sign on front door says room for rent
If you're happy and cheerful room is quite cheap
But beware, I warn you if nasty you'll be
In the cellar company you will keep

I Lift My Glass

I lift my glass to you my friends
And toast a brighter future
For all these wrongs we'll make amends
And start to make things better

So name the drink that you like best
Red wine, white wine or even rosé
Port, beer or spirits and all the rest
I'll take this toast with whatever's on hand

So lift it high and with a mighty cheer
Down the hatch we'll pour it
Over and over we'll toast this my dear
And slowly slide into tomorrow

And through this hazy fog we'll break
With shards of bright light cutting
Time and time again, promises we'll make
But then this damned drink keeps calling

So rack them up, again and again
For it seems we just can't help it
Any excuse that pops in this brain
Is good enough to start drinking

In The Midst Of Night

In the midst of night when all alone
This sadness wraps around me
For all my sins I must atone
And beg them all their forgiveness

Ten thousand angels on pinhead dance
To the sound of an Irish jig
While below in hell devils prance
To wild unbridled passions

He who speaks words of love and peace
Against those that rant for war
Tell them now that war must cease
That all this killing's done

In the depths of jungles deep
Where danger lurks below every tree
There I suggest you do not sleep
Or you may not wake tomorrow

All these things through mind's eye pass
As sleep through my fingers slip
So here my friend, raise wine glass
And I'll toast to a better tomorrow

The Crucifixion
(Multiple Point of View)

GETHSEMANE

It was in the garden of Gethsemane
That he stood there with his men
Judas on his cheek a kiss placed
A sign to soldiers that this was him

The priests their councils they held
To justify their evil ways
Who will witness against this man
For surely he has spoken blasphemy

And Peter sat and watched it all
Then denied knowing Jesus
Three times denied, all in all
Before the cock croweth

In the morning the council they took
To put to death this man Jesus
Bound he was, led away
To Pontius Pilate he was delivered

PONTIUS PILATE

Before me they brought this man
Oh how the priests did hate him
On and on they spoke of Jesus
Accused him of so many things

Are you the King of the Jews?
I asked as he calmly stood there
If you say so, was all he replied
And of nothing else did he speak

All these things the priests accused
Never once did he answer
Stood there all calm and serene
I admit I was astonished

As is wont, when the feast is on
I aim to release a prisoner
But the crowd went wild
For the thief Barabbas they did chant

No matter how I tried to change
The priests whipped up a frenzy
Jesus they wanted crucified
The matter was now beyond me

A bowl of water, I washed my hands
This blood will not stain me
The multitude they thirst for blood
On them and their children be it

SOLDIERS

What sport we had with this one
Handed to us for punishment
His blood flew across the hall
As his body we repeatedly scourged

Stripped him to put on scarlet robe
And a crown of thorns on head
A reed in his right hand
Now, the King of the Jews was ready

We bowed the knee to mock him
Oh Hail King of the Jews
We spat on him repeatedly
And hit him with the reed

All too soon was time to go
His clothes we had to put on him
Time to go on up the hill
Up there he will be crucified

SIMON OF CYRENE

I watch them coming up the street
Burdened by their own heavy crosses
Thieves, murderers, Beggars and such
Out of favour with Roman law

Yet one man he looked so different
Beaten, tortured and so bloody
But from his eyes a light shone forth
One that sent shivers down my spine

This must be the one called Messiah
The one named King of the Jews
So weak that he could barely walk
And constantly kept stumbling

Hey you, a soldier called so harshly
And pointed straight at me
Help this Jew carry his cross
Or it'll not go well with thee

For him I carried this heavy cross
Up to the top of the hill
This place they called Golgotha
A place that reeked of death

CENTURION

Here he was, this one called Jesus
Laid upon the cross made ready
Soldiers there left and right
To drive a spike through his hands

The order was given, hammers fell
The spikes pierced the hands
Feet were crossed and spikes placed
And nailed him to the cross

Up the cross was raised
Pointing to the sky
Above his head a sign did read
Jesus, The King of the Jews

THIEVES

This agony, like nothing before
I'm hanging on a cross
If only I had led a better life
Here I would not be

My friend and I, thieves we are
This way to die our lot
But him, the one called Jesus
What had he done for this

The soldiers here they mocked him so
And so did my friend
I tried to tell him cease and desist
For this was a man of God

Was then he turned and looked at me
Compassion on his face
Through the pain he spoke quite clear
Today you shall be in paradise with me

WOMAN FOLLOWER

How cruel it is to see Jesus
Suffer so much pain
Below his feet some soldiers sat
Gambling for his clothes

The priests and elders stood below
Hurling up abuse
Save thyself if thou canst
For are you not Son of God

On and on they taunted him
Never once letting up
Broke my heart to see this happen
Jesus treated this way

I hear him cry to God his father
As he took upon him all our sins
Breathed his last, the spirit left
And Jesus died that day

The earth it shook
And the sky it darkened
Was then people greatly feared
Truly this was the Son of God

All around me the women wept
As he was taken from the cross
Wrapped in clean linen cloth
And placed in Joseph's tomb

There he lay, his place of rest
This tomb hewn out of rock
The entrance of the tomb secure
A great stone rolled across the door

MARY MAGDALENE

We have lost him, we lost Jesus
How could this possibly be
Sadly I and Mary
Made our way to the tomb

The earth it shook
And there was an angel
His face like lightning
And garment white as snow

There he sat upon the rock
No longer across the door
Fear not, he quietly spoke
Him you seek is no longer here

Did Jesus not tell to you
That death would have no hold
Three days he lay in tomb
But now he's back again

With fear and joy we raced away
To find all the disciples
Back they came to see for themselves
This tomb that stood so empty

On the way they were met by Jesus
They cried and worshipped him
Tell them all to go to Galilee
And there they shall all see me

Sane Inside My Insanity

Howling wind through the barren wasteland of my mind
I scream, and the scream echoes over and over
Ripped to shreds by the violent putrid wind
And the tatters still hang there fading into eternity

I am here a prisoner behind these bloodshot eyes
Can you not see me? can you not hear my silent screams?
Begging to be set free, allowed to escape my captivity
I am locked in this shell, they pretend I am insane

Arms and legs are covered in scars, it was not I
They must have done it, although they claim I cut myself
I see the cuts and I can faintly recall seeing the blade
Slowly slicing, skin parting, the blood slowly welling

It was not my hand that held the knife, not I that cut
It was another, they wish to hurt me, to drive me crazy
Please I need help, save me before they return
I can feel the walls closing in again, too late, too late

Conned By Death

In the middle of the night I was awoken
By my bed this figure dark and scary
Robes of black and with scythe in hand
I thought that surely my time had come

You're safe, he said with gravelly voice
If a favour you'll do for me tonight
Can't remember when last I had a break
A holiday is what I really need

My knees were knocking ever so loudly
A terror had come over me
If I said no, then what would happen
Something I really did not want to see

I nodded yes and as quick as a flash
Was suddenly dressed in black
I'll be back said he with a smile
Now looking ever so normal

Been doing this job for I don't know
Seems to be like centuries
Forgot to ask how long he'd be
I think death has somehow conned me

Beware, for one of these nights
At your bed I'll be standing

Love Lies Dying

Days are filled with lonely nights
And nights are cold and barren
Then I dream these dreams of you
Of a life left so far behind me

All these lies you told to cover lust
Your lust not for me but someone other
It seems that in the stakes of love
My call you would not answer

I can understand if love was lost
No longer there between us
Why these lies to cover all up
That your heart now belongs to another

So take the joy that once we had
The trust, the hopes and all the dreams
Pack it in with the future we had
And take all these things with you

I'd rather spend my nights alone
Than to live a life of lies
At least I know somewhere, sometime
I'll find a love that's mine

The Narrow Path

This narrow path, rocky and steep
So hard to travel on
Legs aching and feet so sore
They're all covered in blisters

I look to the left and a highway I see
So wide, smooth, and inviting
Tempted I am to jump across
To ease my journey slightly

But then I think, let's wait and see
This next hill I'll be climbing
I wonder if the other side
Will show me what's awaiting

The crest I reach and there below
A massive gate, the entrance into Heaven
Angels dancing all around
And echoes of their rejoicing

I look to see the highway's end
Disappearing in a crevice
Sulphur fumes and flames shoot out
And the wail of souls tormented

How glad and blessed I am
That narrow path I stayed on
For now the journey's end I've reached
And celebrating in Heaven

The Planet Frazzle

In another universe in another dimension
Is the planet Frazzle where live the Frazzlers

It does not matter what time of day
It does not matter what time of night
All they ever want to do is frazzle
Not that there is anything wrong with that

But......................................

Frazzle is the very first thing in the morning
Frazzle is the very last thing at night
And, yes, frazzle all day and night long
Well, it is just downright frazzling

There is no misery or strife
No wars or even any minor conflicts
There was just no time left over for any of that

It was frazzle this or frazzle that
Frazzle anything they wanted
On the good old planet Frazzle

The Hand

I think I'm seeing things
I must be hallucinating
I see a hand on the road
Not attached to anything

Finger stuck up in the air
A gesture quite so rude
What is this hand doing here
And why is it rudely pointing

Over I walk to pick it up
But quickly it runs away
Is this a hoax or movie stunt
Around I look for cameras

Nothing there, it all seems fine
Yet the hand is still around
This time it makes a hollow fist
And rudely moves around

Slowly I took of my coat
Pretended to be indifferent
With one quick flick
I flung it over this rotten hand

Got you now, you rude mongrel
Wrapped him tightly in my coat
If you're the owner of this hand
To have it back you're welcome

To find me you will know how
But a finder's fee I'll be expecting

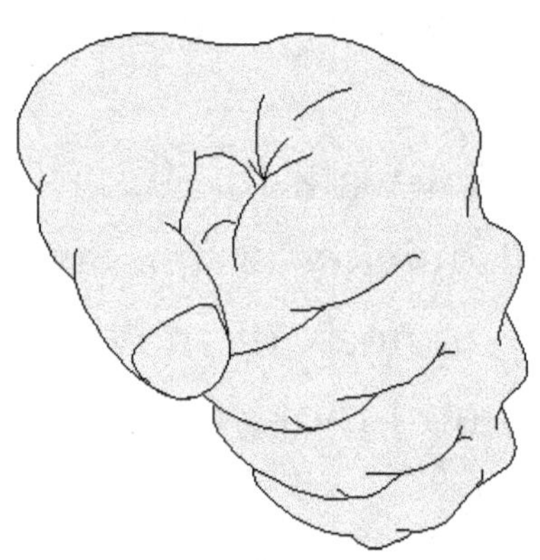

Cheating Death

Death stood there at my door
Black robes in wind flapping
Scythe in hand with moon's glint
Dead black eyes at me staring

Not every day, as you might know
That Death comes on you calling
But when he does, time is up
To the world goodbye you're saying

A bony finger pointed at me
Then poked me in the chest
"Time to go, your life is up
Your soul is mine to take"

Sweat was running down my brow
Not ready yet for dying
But to run away won't work
No-one has outrun Death yet

"Come inside, I'll make you a drink"
I thought just to stall him
Surprisingly he nodded his head
And inside me he followed

"Beer or wine or spirits too
Which one will you choose?"
Death pointed at Glenfiddich
The best whisky that I had

What the hell, I might as well
No taking it with me
Poured myself a single shot
And for Death a triple

We drank for some hours
While he told me of his woes
This terrible job of souls collecting
And no-one anywhere to call as friend

Now I must admit that I felt sorry
But not quite sorry enough
When he fell asleep on my lounge
The page with my name I removed

Morning time when he checked his book
He was puzzled why he came here
Said goodbye, went on his way
That was near on two thousand years ago

How I long for death to come and call
To end this, my sad existence
Seek in the shadows here and there
Hoping that I might just find him

I've kept the page all these years
I want to give it to him
If he comes to visit you
Please tell him about me

Through The Mirror

Through the mirror I did stride
And met my evil self
There he was on the other side
As bold as you could please

"What brings you here?"
He spoke, a snarl upon his face
"Go, leave, or I'll turn you
Into another one like me"

Face to face I stood with me
And liked not what I saw
Could this me be like me
This side that was so evil

Quickly now I strode back round
To leave my evil me
I had stood and faced myself
Was shocked at what I'd seen

Could we all have this evil side
This battle for control
I can see him watching me
He's locked up so tight

Given a chance he'd race right out
And fight me for control

A Male Monologue

Forgive me my friends for what I have done
The unimaginable horrors I've created
Loneliness drove me relentlessly onwards
To achieve this unholy created abomination

Far into the night I worked so often
Cared not, bright light or gloomy corners
Bits of animals gathered in the forest
Mattered not how long they lay dead

For months I worked assembling pieces
Stitching, sewing, gluing and screwing bits
Ever so slowly the shape made sense
I was almost finished, creating it

Needed lots of power to get it going
Normal electricity was not be enough
Hooked it up to my Ford Mustang
Had an Aston Martin V12 engine

Pushed the pedal hard to the floor
At one eighty creature started shaking
That was good, was almost alive
At two sixty creature fired, it was alive

Hit the skids and came to stop
Creature easily came right up
Took it home but then trouble started
Opened mouth and out it poured

On and on I could not stop it
From it's mouth hurled strange abuse
"Change your clothes, your shirt is dirty
Wash the dishes , make the bed"

"No more beer, you've drunk too much
Why you always watching football
There is so much work outside
Mow the lawn, do the weeding"

Now I don't know what to do
I've created, it seems, a monster
It seems that name it I must
So be it, I will call it woe-man

Called it woe-man because all the woe
It will bring to us poor men
Though the outside is so gorgeous
Inside is stuffed full of man's woe

So forgive me all my friends
I've loosened this creature upon you
And so rapidly it multiplies
Soon it will hold the upper hand

So again I beg forgive me
As I go to the silent grave
Please don't bury a woman near me
Or I'll never hear THE END

Get Out Of Hell Free

I admit that I'm no good
I steal, lie and cheat
It's better to take than to give
That's my philosophy

Out I'm walking, through the park
Looking to make a quick buck
Snatch a bag or lift a wallet
But I'd draw the line at mugging

Saw two guys kicking a dog
Putting in boots and all
Then I realised for goodness sake
Was an old wrinkled woman

"Help me," she cried, "please help me
They're going to kill me"
What the hell, don't want to know
But she could be my own Granny

I'm gonna regret this I know
But in I stepped to stop it
Copped a few on my face
Before I sent them fleeing

Helped her up, what a mess
Her face was all bloody
"Here son, thank you," she said
And pressed a card in my hand

Before I could say anything
Off she ran, sprightly for an oldie
Looked at the card, what a joke
Get 'Out Of Hell Free' card

Was going to toss it in the bin
But then stuck it in my pocket
This night's a bummer, heading home
Tomorrow surely will be better

Crossing road I hear a noise
Bloody idiot, bearing down on me
Over the bonnet and over the roof
Into the air I'm sent flying

At first there's pain, such pain
Then it eases and settles
I thought bloody idiotic driver
Then I saw my body laying there

Through the ground I suddenly dropped
Right through to the depths of Hell
Demons here all around
I've passed the point of panic

A demon came up, right up to me
Behold a sight so terrible
"You'll be mine for eternity
And the torture will have you screaming"

His whip lashed out
The pain so fierce
I screamed and screamed in agony
He raised his whip to lash again

Was then I remembered card I had
Quickly held out card to show
Demon cursed and fire spat
Said, "I'll return you to the surface"

I opened eyes and saw the park
Was this a dream I dreamt
Looked at card and on it said
This card has been redeemed

Now I don't know if this is true
And I was down in Hell
But across my back still wear the mark
Such as one made by a whip

I thank God that mercy I showed
To that poor old lady
For maybe she was, and I believe
An angel in disguise

Not Just A Number

A baby's born into this world
It's fat and round and jolly
Eyes wide in wonderment
A whole world awaiting

Baby boy is soon a youth
A pride and joy for parents
Many plans for future made
He dreams of being a doctor

The youth a man to war must go
To fight a foreign battle
Face in sand life slips away
A casualty, a number

When will you see what we have lost
That these are not just numbers
Each a life so unique
There will never be another

Dark Of Night

In the dark of night it slithers past
So quietly you can barely hear
Where is it heading? what does it seek?
These questions need some answers

And then it hides under the bed
Where it looks and quietly listens
Then a quick dash under the stairs
Around the corner it's peeking

Into the kitchen and under the sink
Ready to journey onwards
Slither left and slither right
And out the back door open

Into the garden it disappears
Among the red rose planted
And then it's gone without a sound
Until the early morning

Carnival

The sun beats down on city streets
A haze of heat lays over
Concrete beast it barely stirs
It is too much lethargic

On setting sun the beast it stirs
Awakening, reviving
People throng the streets around
And gaily are they costumed

Music starts from here and there
And in the air it mixes
Calypso band and jazz combine
And rock n' roll then join them

Parade of floats come passing by
With Sinbad and his sailors
Fairies, dragons, princess' and elves
And so many others beside them

The floats pass by for about an hour
Oh what a mixture of things to see
The crowd shouts in their excitement
The carnival is here

Homeless

Oh the hate and anger there
The pain and mistrust
Fist in pocket, tightly clenched
Shoulders round and hunched

What in life has made you this
Brought you such despair
The suffering carved on your face
So plain for all to see

Clothes are ragged, dirty too
A bottle your best friend
Sleep on benches where you can
No place to call a home

How I wish that I could help
Yet help you soundly scorn
A meal, a drink, is all you want
For the rest you could not care

Hell Of A Ride

Sadness, gladness, pain and gain
These are words used again and again

Where does that leave you when you want to hide
When life has taken you on a hell of a ride

You've had enough of the sadness and pain
But will you get chance for the gladness and gain

You need to ask will you risk it all
Toss the dice and go for the long haul

So is the answer do you take this chance
So the answer could be a lifelong romance

Sit With Me

Oh my child who weeps at night
And feels so all alone
Know that in my sight you are
A creature perfect born

Your blemishes they disappear
With robes of spotless white
Know the love that covers you
And all your Father's might

All good things I want for you
That Heaven has to offer
So cry no more you child of God
Your Father's love does cover

Rejoice to know your heritage
In Heaven is waiting
Sit with me at my right hand
Together there forever

The King Of The Jews

Slowly He raised His weary head
And glanced about the room
Mocking eyes stared back at Him
"Are you the King of the Jews?"
"If you say so," He answered them
And nothing else He spoke

"What with this man shall we do?"
The man called Pilate asked
The crowd was primed
The answer swift
A chant did arise
"Crucify, crucify, the King of Jews"

Soldiers came to lead Him out
Into a hall so great
Robes of purple on His back
And thorns they used for crown
"Hail the King of Jews," they mocked
And spat while bending knee

A cross was given for Him to bear
To drag it through the town
Soldiers sneered to move Him on
As people lined the streets
Come to see the man they called
The King of the Jews

Top of the hill they reached
The place to do the deed
The cross on the ground they threw
His body placed on there
Nails pierced His hands and feet
His agony so great

Upright the cross was lifted
For all to come and see
Robber right and robber left
Were crucified with Him
And on His cross was written
So all might see and know
The King of the Jews

The hours dragged, the sun was hot
The priests were mocking Him
"Come show us signs and wonders
Descend now from the cross
Save yourself, King of Jews
If you be such a man"

The sun it hid it's face to weep
And darkness filled the land
The man upon the cross cried out
"My God, My God
Why hast thou forsaken me"
And then He breathed His last

The women wept, the man was dead
His body wrapped in linen
This tomb in rock, prepared for Joseph
Now becomes His resting place
A stone to seal the entrance

Three days had passed
Their grief still fresh
The women came to anoint Him
To their surprise and unbelief
The stone unsealed the entrance

Into the tomb they quickly raced
To find an angel therein
"Be not alarmed," said he
"The one you seek has risen"

The Word made flesh
The living God
Jesus Christ
The Saviour

Fright

Tell me, can you help me
I'm in such a fright
Demons come howling
Round my bedpost at night

I squirm and scream
And turn on the light
See demons clearer now
What a terrible sight

They howl and caper
Show their claws and fangs
Dripping, drooling
Ready to take a bite

Then I awake
Dripping with sweat
It was only a dream
But...what was that?

Regret

If I could only turn back time
And live my life again
What are the things I would change?
My regrets and discontentments

There's many times that I can pick
Where choices were the bad ones
People hurt and left behind
The choice now not so simple

And yet if back I manage to go
So much of now be missing
Bittersweet memories of things gone past
Are blended with the present

If I could only turn back time
And live my life again
But then I look at life I have now
And wouldn't want to change it

My Friend

Many people come and go
Not all that touch you
You my friend have touched me deep
A stirring in my soul

When I'm down and misery hits
You are the one I count on
A cheerful smile, encouraging word
And soon I'm feeling better

When I'm wrong and really mess up
You are there to support me
Never once do you criticise
A sign of true friendship

So when I lay late at night
Staring at the ceiling
My thanks I give to the Lord
For sending me your friendship

Why I Love You

Why do I love you? you ask me
As we run around the playground
Let me think, I'll answer you
Before the bell rings to go to classes
Well your face has less pimples
Than your sisters Clara and Jane
Your chewing gum you will share
And your deodorant hides the smell
You'd never know you shower weekly
You've got the biggest breasts in class
And they bounce rather nicely
You don't scream if my hand should slip
To touch those gorgeous boobies
And you don't call me stinky pervert
Not like those other girls do
You're the only girl I know
I can get close enough to kiss ya
I love the short skirts you wear
I can see your pink knickers
You don't mind if I copy at tests
And you even do my homework
There goes the bell, we better go
Before the teachers come looking

Sounds Of Despair

Tears of blood drip from my soul
And stain the virgin's table
Food it touches rotten turns
And carrion eaters come to devour

High pitched sound of breaking heart
Shatters all the windows
Leaving open for doom to fly in
And spread it's misery round

The pounding of brain tormented
Sets up vibrations all around
It breaks all the foundations
Sends my reality crumbling down

The cry of utter loneliness
Echoes back as my despair
For left I have all of nothing
'Cause you took all that was there

Clip, Clop

I sit and watch it all
On the sheltered side
Fungus grows on the trees
Where the sun don't shine
From deep in the woods
So fast for to get back home
The horse did trot
Clip, clop, clip, clop
The horse did trot
So fast for to get back home
From deep in the woods
Where the sun don't shine
Fungus grows on trees
On the sheltered side
I sit and watch it all